The Bold Navigator:

Mastering Investment Success Amidst Uncertainty

Daniel C. Partin

Table of content

Introduction

Welcome to the world of investment, where uncertainty and opportunity intertwine, and where the bold navigator thrives. In this book, "The Bold Navigator: Mastering Investment Success Amidst Uncertainty," I, Daniel invite you on a transformative journey through the complex and ever-evolving landscape of investing.

As a seasoned investor and financial strategist, I have spent decades honing my skills and deepening my understanding of the markets. Throughout my career, I have weathered the storms of uncertainty, navigated turbulent waters, and emerged triumphant. My experiences have molded me into a knowledgeable and astute practitioner, and I am thrilled to share the wisdom I have gained with you.

Investing is an art, an intricate dance between risk and reward, and I firmly believe that success in this realm is not merely a matter of luck. It is a carefully cultivated skill, driven by meticulous research, thoughtful analysis, and the courage to act decisively when others hesitate. It is the ability to seize opportunities amid the chaos, to remain calm in the face of volatility, and to adapt swiftly to a rapidly changing world.

In "The Bold Navigator," I aim to empower you, the reader, to become a master of investment success in even the most uncertain times. Whether you are a seasoned investor looking to refine your strategies or a newcomer eager to embark on your investment journey, this book will provide you with the knowledge and tools necessary to thrive amidst the unpredictable nature of the financial markets.

Throughout these pages, I will share my hard-earned insights, guiding you through the fundamental principles of investing and revealing the secrets of navigating ambiguity with confidence. You will discover how to identify and evaluate investment opportunities, mitigate risk, and make informed decisions that align with your financial goals. Additionally, I will equip you with strategies to manage your emotions, conquer fear and greed, and maintain a long-term perspective, enabling you to navigate the inevitable ups and downs of the market with grace and resilience.

Drawing from my own triumphs and failures, I will also explore real-life case studies, illustrating the principles and strategies discussed in this book. These stories will bring to life the lessons learned and provide valuable perspectives on the application of the bold navigator's mindset.

In a world that is constantly evolving, where disruptive technologies emerge, geopolitical tensions unfold, and global markets fluctuate, it is crucial to cultivate a mindset that thrives amidst uncertainty. By embracing the principles shared within these pages, you will unlock the power to adapt, innovate, and capitalize on the ever-changing investment landscape.

I invite you to join me on this transformative journey—a journey that will not only enhance your investment acumen but also empower you to become a bold navigator in all areas of your life. Together, we will seize the opportunities that lie within the unknown and master the art of investment success amidst uncertainty.

So, prepare to embark on this exhilarating expedition into the world of investing. Let us navigate uncharted waters, embrace ambiguity, and emerge as masters of our financial destinies. The bold navigator within you is waiting to be awakened, and I am honored to be your guide on this remarkable voyage.

Navigating the Investment Landscape: Embracing Uncertainty as an Opportunity

Navigating the investment landscape can be a challenging task, especially in an environment characterized by uncertainty. However, instead of viewing uncertainty as a barrier, successful investors embrace it as an opportunity to make informed decisions and potentially generate higher returns. We will explore the concept of navigating the investment landscape by embracing uncertainty.

Understanding uncertainty:
Uncertainty refers to the lack of predictability and the presence of risks and unknown factors in the investment landscape. These uncertainties can arise from various sources, such as geopolitical events, economic conditions, technological advancements, and market volatility. It is

essential to recognize that uncertainty is an inherent part of investing and cannot be completely eliminated.

Embracing uncertainty as an opportunity: Instead of fearing uncertainty, successful investors perceive it as a chance to identify undervalued assets, capitalize on market inefficiencies, and outperform the broader market. They understand that uncertainty creates price fluctuations and market dislocations that can be exploited for profit.

Developing a long-term investment strategy: Embracing uncertainty requires adopting a long-term investment strategy rather than attempting to time the market or chase short-term gains. A long-term approach allows investors to ride out market fluctuations and take advantage of compounding returns over time. It also provides the flexibility to adjust the investment portfolio as new information becomes available.

Conducting thorough research: In uncertain times, it becomes even more critical to conduct extensive research and due diligence on potential investment opportunities. This involves analyzing financial statements, understanding industry trends, evaluating competitive advantages, and assessing management capabilities. By gathering as much information as possible, investors can make more informed decisions based on fundamentals rather than short-term market sentiment.

Diversification: Diversification is a fundamental principle of investment management and plays a vital role in navigating uncertainty. By spreading investments across different asset classes, industries, and geographical regions, investors can reduce risk and protect their portfolios from the impact of unforeseen events. Diversification provides a buffer against potential losses in specific investments while allowing for potential gains in others.

Risk management: Embracing uncertainty does not mean ignoring risk. Successful investors proactively manage risk by setting clear investment objectives, establishing risk tolerance levels, and implementing appropriate risk management strategies. This may include using stop-loss orders, hedging with derivatives, or allocating assets based on risk-reward profiles.

Staying informed and adaptable: Embracing uncertainty requires staying informed about market developments, global trends, and emerging risks. Investors should keep a close eye on economic indicators, policy changes, technological advancements, and shifts in consumer behavior. Being adaptable and willing to adjust investment strategies based on new information is crucial in navigating the ever-changing investment landscape.

Seeking professional advice: Navigating uncertainty can be complex, and seeking professional advice from financial advisors, portfolio managers, or investment professionals can provide valuable insights and guidance. Professionals with expertise in analyzing market conditions and managing investments can help investors make better-informed decisions aligned with their financial goals.

Maintaining a disciplined approach: Embracing uncertainty as an opportunity requires discipline and emotional resilience. Market volatility and unexpected events can trigger emotional responses, leading to irrational investment decisions. By maintaining a disciplined approach, adhering to a well-thought-out investment strategy, and avoiding reactionary behavior, investors can better navigate the ups and downs of the investment landscape.

Understanding Risk: Building a Solid Foundation for Investment Success

Understanding risk is crucial when it comes to building a solid foundation for investment success. Investing inherently involves taking risks, and without a proper understanding of risk, investors may make hasty decisions, suffer significant losses, and fail to achieve their financial goals.

1. Definition of Risk:

Risk in investments refers to the potential for loss or variability in returns that may deviate from the expected outcome. It arises from uncertainties in the financial markets, economic conditions, company performance, regulatory changes, and other factors that can affect the value of an investment.

2. **Types of Risk**:
There are several types of risks that investors should consider:

a) **Market Risk**: Also known as systematic risk, it is the risk associated with overall market movements. Factors such as economic conditions, geopolitical events, interest rates, and market sentiment can impact the value of all investments.

b) **Specific Risk**: Also called unsystematic risk, it is the risk specific to a particular investment or asset. It can include factors like company management, industry-specific events, competitive landscape, and regulatory changes that affect a particular investment's value.

c) **Credit Risk**: It refers to the risk of default by borrowers or issuers of debt instruments, such as bonds. If a borrower fails to repay their debt obligations, investors may face a loss of principal or interest payments.

d) **Liquidity Risk**: It is the risk of not being able to buy or sell an investment quickly at a fair price. Investments with low liquidity may have wider bid-ask spreads, and investors may face challenges in converting their holdings into cash.

e) **Inflation Risk**: Inflation erodes the purchasing power of money over time. Investments with returns that do not outpace inflation can result in a decrease in real value.

f) **Currency Risk**: This risk arises when investing in assets denominated in foreign currencies. Fluctuations in exchange rates can affect the value of investments and the returns when converted back to the investor's base currency.

3. **Measurement of Risk**:

Measuring risk is essential for investors to assess and compare various investment opportunities. Here are some commonly used methods to measure risk:

a) **Standard Deviation**: It measures the historical volatility of an investment's returns. Higher standard deviation implies greater variability and higher risk.

b) **Beta:** Beta measures an investment's sensitivity to market movements. A beta of 1 indicates the investment moves in line with the market, while a beta greater than 1 implies higher volatility.

c) **Value at Risk (VaR):** VaR estimates the maximum potential loss a portfolio may experience within a specified confidence level over a given time horizon.

d) **Risk-adjusted Return Measures**: Ratios such as Sharpe ratio and Treynor ratio assess the risk-adjusted performance of an investment by considering the return earned per unit of risk taken.

4. Risk Management Strategies: Managing risk is crucial for protecting investments and minimizing potential losses. Here are some strategies commonly employed by investors:

1. **Diversification**: Diversification involves spreading investments across different asset classes, sectors, industries, geographical regions, and even individual securities. The primary goal of diversification is to reduce the risk associated with a specific investment or group of investments. By diversifying, investors can minimize the impact of any single investment's poor performance on the overall portfolio.

Here are some key points to consider regarding diversification:

a. **Asset Classes**: Diversification starts with allocating investments across different asset classes such as stocks, bonds, cash, real estate, commodities, and alternative investments like hedge funds or private equity. Each asset class has its own risk and return characteristics, so holding a mix of them helps reduce exposure to any one asset class's volatility.

b. **Sectors and Industries**: Within the equity portion of a portfolio, diversification can be achieved by investing across various sectors and industries. Different sectors perform differently in various market conditions, so having exposure to multiple sectors helps reduce the impact of a downturn in any single sector.

c. **Geographical Diversification**: Investing in different regions and countries helps mitigate the risk associated with any single country's economic or political issues.

Global diversification allows investors to benefit from growth opportunities across different markets.

d. **Individual Securities**: When investing in stocks or bonds, diversification can be achieved by holding a broad range of individual securities. By avoiding excessive concentration in a few stocks or bonds, investors can reduce the risk of significant losses due to the poor performance of a single company or issuer.

e. **Correlation**: While diversification is important, it is essential to consider the correlation between assets. Ideally, investments should have low or negative correlation, meaning their prices move independently of each other. Low correlation enhances the benefits of diversification as losses in one investment may be offset by gains in another.

2. **Asset Allocation**:
Asset allocation is the process of determining the optimal mix of different asset classes in a portfolio based on an investor's goals, risk tolerance, and investment horizon. It is a strategic decision that balances risk and return.
Here are some key considerations for asset allocation:

a. **Risk Tolerance**: Investors should assess their risk tolerance, which refers to their ability and willingness to tolerate fluctuations in the value of their investments. Risk tolerance depends on factors such as investment goals, time horizon, financial situation, and personal temperament. Aggressive investors may have a higher allocation to stocks, while conservative investors may lean towards bonds and cash.

b. **Investment Goals**: Different investment goals, such as retirement planning, saving for a down payment on a house, or funding a child's education, require different asset allocation strategies. Longer-term goals generally allow for more aggressive asset allocations since there is more time to recover from market downturns.

c. **Rebalancing**: Asset allocation is not a one-time decision. Over time, the performance of different asset classes may deviate from the initial allocation, resulting in an unbalanced portfolio. Regularly rebalancing the portfolio brings it back to the desired asset allocation, ensuring that it aligns with the investor's risk profile and goals.

d. **Investment Horizon:** The length of time an investor plans to hold their investments influences asset allocation decisions. Longer investment horizons generally allow for a higher allocation to growth-oriented assets like stocks, as there is more time to weather short-term volatility and potentially benefit from long-term growth.

e. **Diversification within Asset Classes:** Asset allocation also involves diversifying within each asset class. For example, within the equity portion, investors can allocate funds across large-cap, mid-cap, and small-cap stocks, as well as domestic and international equities. Similarly, within bonds

3. Stop loss orders

Stop loss orders are an essential tool used by investors and traders to manage risk and protect their investment positions. A stop loss order is a predetermined instruction given to a broker or a trading platform to sell a security when it reaches a specified price level. The primary purpose of a stop loss order is to limit potential losses and minimize the impact of adverse market movements.

Here are some key points to consider when discussing stop loss orders:

Risk management: Stop loss orders are primarily used for risk management. By setting a predetermined exit point, investors can limit their potential losses if the price of a security moves against their position. This helps investors maintain discipline and stick to their predefined risk tolerance levels.

Types of stop loss orders:

a. **Market stop loss order**: This type of order is executed at the best available market price once the specified stop price is reached. However, the execution price may differ from the stop price during volatile market conditions.

b. **Limit stop loss order:** This order is executed at a specific price or better after the stop price is reached. It ensures that the investor does not sell the security at a price worse than the limit price, providing a greater control over the execution price.

c. **Trailing stop loss order**: This type of order is dynamic and adjusts the stop price as the market price moves in the investor's favor. It helps capture profits while still providing protection against downside risk.

Determining stop loss levels: Deciding the appropriate stop loss level can be challenging and depends on various factors, including an investor's risk tolerance, investment strategy, time horizon, and market volatility. Technical analysis tools such as support and resistance levels, moving averages, or trendlines can be used to identify potential stop loss levels.

Psychological impact: Stop loss orders can help investors overcome emotional biases and make rational decisions. Fear and greed often drive investors to hold losing positions for too long or sell winning positions too quickly. Setting a stop loss level in advance removes the emotional component from the decision-making process.

Volatility and execution risk: During periods of high volatility, such as market opening or major news announcements, stop loss orders may be subject to slippage. Slippage occurs when the execution price of the order differs from the stop price, leading to potential losses or reduced gains. It's important to consider market conditions and liquidity when setting stop loss levels.

False breakouts and whipsaws: In certain market conditions, prices may briefly breach a stop loss level before reversing and moving in the desired direction. This can result in premature exits and missed opportunities. Traders often use additional technical indicators or confirmatory signals to filter out false breakouts and reduce the likelihood of being stopped out prematurely.

Monitoring and adjusting stop loss orders: Market conditions can change rapidly, so it's important to regularly monitor and adjust stop loss orders accordingly. As prices move in a favorable direction, trailing stop loss orders can be adjusted to lock in profits and protect against potential reversals.

Limitations and risks: While stop loss orders provide a valuable risk management tool, they have some limitations. During extreme market conditions, such as market gaps or rapid price declines, stop loss orders may not execute at the desired price level, resulting in larger losses than anticipated (known as slippage risk). Additionally, relying solely on stop loss orders without considering other fundamental or technical factors may not be sufficient for making well-informed investment decisions.

.

The Power of Knowledge: Research and Due Diligence in Uncertain Times

The power of knowledge, research, and due diligence is crucial in uncertain times. In an ever-changing world where information is abundant but not always reliable, having the ability to navigate through the noise and make informed decisions becomes essential. Whether it's in personal matters, business ventures, or even societal issues, the application of knowledge and thorough research can lead to better outcomes and mitigate risks.

Research serves as the foundation for acquiring knowledge and understanding a subject matter. It involves the systematic investigation of a particular topic, using various sources and methodologies to gather information, analyze data, and draw conclusions. Research provides a solid framework for decision-making, enabling individuals or organizations to make well-informed choices based on evidence rather than assumptions or speculation.

In uncertain times, when the future is unpredictable and circumstances are volatile, research becomes even more critical. It helps in assessing risks and identifying potential opportunities. By examining past trends, current market conditions, and analyzing relevant data, researchers can gain insights into potential outcomes, enabling them to plan and adapt accordingly. For example, businesses conducting market research during uncertain economic times can identify emerging trends, consumer preferences, and potential shifts in demand, allowing them to adjust their strategies and offerings to stay ahead of the competition.

Furthermore, research and due diligence are vital for minimizing risks and avoiding costly mistakes. When uncertainty is high, making impulsive or uninformed decisions can have severe consequences. By thoroughly investigating a situation, analyzing available information, and considering different perspectives, individuals and organizations can uncover potential pitfalls and make more accurate risk assessments. This approach reduces the likelihood of making hasty decisions that may lead to financial losses or other negative outcomes.

The power of knowledge, research, and due diligence extends beyond personal decision-making. In the broader context of societal issues, these elements play a significant role in shaping policies, addressing complex problems, and advancing collective understanding. In uncertain times, policymakers rely on research to assess the impact of various interventions, develop evidence-based policies, and anticipate the consequences of their decisions. By relying on research, they can better understand the challenges at hand, evaluate potential solutions, and make informed choices that serve the best interests of society as a whole.

However, it's important to acknowledge that research and knowledge alone are not sufficient. Critical thinking, analytical skills, and the ability to discern reliable information from misinformation are equally essential. With the rise of fake news, biased sources, and manipulated data, it's crucial to approach information with a healthy dose of skepticism. Fact-checking, verifying sources, and considering multiple perspectives are vital to ensure that the knowledge acquired is accurate and trustworthy.

The power of knowledge, research, and due diligence is invaluable in uncertain times. It empowers individuals, businesses, and policymakers to make informed decisions, navigate through uncertainties, and adapt to changing circumstances. Research provides a solid foundation for understanding complex issues, assessing risks, and identifying opportunities. By leveraging the power of knowledge, individuals and organizations can better position themselves for success and contribute to the advancement of society as a whole.

Mastering Market Psychology: Staying Calm Amidst Market Volatility

Mastering market psychology and staying calm amidst market volatility are crucial skills for investors and traders. Market volatility refers to the rapid and significant price fluctuations in financial markets, often driven by various factors such as economic events, geopolitical tensions, and investor sentiment. It can create a high level of uncertainty and emotions among market participants, leading to impulsive decision-making and potentially harmful financial outcomes.

To effectively navigate market volatility and maintain a calm mindset, it is essential to understand and address the psychological aspects that influence investor behavior. Here are several key points to consider:

Emotional intelligence: Emotional intelligence involves recognizing and managing one's emotions effectively. Successful investors cultivate self-awareness and emotional control to avoid making impulsive decisions based on fear, greed, or panic. They understand that emotions can cloud judgment and lead to irrational behavior, impacting investment outcomes.

Long-term perspective: One effective strategy for staying calm during market volatility is adopting a long-term perspective. Understanding that markets experience ups and downs over time helps investors avoid reacting impulsively to short-term fluctuations. Focusing on the bigger picture and the fundamental value of investments can provide stability and reduce anxiety during periods of volatility.

Risk tolerance assessment: Knowing one's risk tolerance is crucial for managing market volatility. Investors must evaluate their financial goals, time horizon, and ability to withstand potential losses. By aligning investments with their risk tolerance, individuals can minimize the likelihood of making panic-driven decisions during turbulent market conditions.

Diversification: Diversification is a risk management technique that involves spreading investments across different asset classes, sectors, and regions. This strategy helps reduce the impact of volatility on a portfolio, as losses in one area may be offset by gains in others. Diversification can contribute to a calmer investing experience by mitigating the negative effects of concentrated positions.

Investment discipline and strategy: Establishing an investment discipline and sticking to a well-defined strategy is crucial during market volatility. This involves conducting thorough research, setting realistic expectations, and following predetermined rules for buying and selling investments. By adhering to a disciplined approach, investors can avoid making hasty decisions driven by short-term market fluctuations.

Continuous learning: Markets are complex and constantly evolving. Engaging in ongoing education and staying informed about economic indicators, industry trends, and geopolitical events can provide a better understanding of market dynamics. The more knowledge and information an investor possesses, the more confident and less prone to panic they are likely to be in volatile situations.

Seeking professional advice: Investors who feel overwhelmed by market volatility or lack the time and expertise to manage their investments may benefit from seeking professional advice. Financial advisors or investment professionals can provide guidance, help formulate an investment plan aligned with individual goals, and offer reassurance during turbulent market periods.

Maintaining a balanced mindset: Developing a balanced mindset involves maintaining realistic expectations and accepting that market volatility is an inherent part of investing. Understanding that both ups and downs are part of the investment journey can help investors remain composed during turbulent periods.

Strategies for Uncertain Markets: Adapting and Thriving in Changing Environments

Adapting and thriving in uncertain markets is a significant challenge for businesses in today's dynamic and rapidly changing environments. Uncertainty can arise due to various factors such as technological advancements, economic fluctuations, regulatory changes, political instability, and shifts in consumer preferences. To navigate these uncertain markets successfully, businesses need to develop and implement effective strategies that allow them to adapt quickly and thrive amidst volatility. We will explore some key strategies that can help businesses in uncertain markets.

Flexibility and Agility: In uncertain markets, being flexible and agile is crucial. Businesses should be prepared to adjust their strategies, products, and services rapidly based on emerging trends and changing customer demands. This may involve revisiting business models, streamlining processes, and fostering a culture of innovation and experimentation.

Market Research and Analysis: In uncertain markets, accurate and up-to-date market research becomes even more critical. Businesses should invest in comprehensive market research and analysis to gain a deep understanding of customer needs, preferences, and behavior. This information will help them identify new opportunities, anticipate market shifts, and make informed decisions.

Diversification: Diversification is a strategy that involves expanding the range of products, services, or markets served by a business. By diversifying, companies can reduce their reliance on a single product or market and spread their risks. This strategy allows businesses to tap into new revenue streams and adapt to changing market conditions more effectively.

Innovation and Continuous Improvement: In uncertain markets, innovation is essential for survival and growth. Companies should foster a culture of innovation that encourages employees to generate new ideas, experiment with new technologies, and develop creative solutions. Continuous improvement processes, such as Lean or Six Sigma, can help identify inefficiencies and optimize operations, enhancing the company's adaptability.

Strategic Partnerships and Collaborations: Forming strategic partnerships and collaborations can be beneficial in uncertain markets. By leveraging the expertise and resources of other organizations, businesses can enhance their capabilities, access new markets, and mitigate risks. Collaborations can also foster knowledge sharing and enable businesses to respond more effectively to market changes.

Scenario Planning: Scenario planning involves developing multiple plausible scenarios for the future and analyzing their potential impact on the business. By considering a range of possible outcomes, businesses can better prepare for different market conditions and develop contingency plans. Scenario planning helps identify potential risks and opportunities, enabling businesses to respond proactively.

Customer Focus and Customer Relationship Management: In uncertain markets, maintaining a strong focus on customers becomes crucial. Businesses should invest in building strong relationships with their customers, understanding their evolving needs, and delivering superior customer experiences. Customer relationship management (CRM) tools and strategies can help gather customer data, personalize interactions, and build long-term loyalty.

Financial Prudence and Risk Management: Uncertain markets often bring financial risks. Businesses should practice prudent financial management by maintaining adequate cash reserves, diversifying their investment portfolios, and managing debt levels. Implementing robust risk management practices, such as hedging strategies or insurance coverage, can help mitigate potential financial risks.

Talent Management and Employee Engagement: A skilled and motivated workforce is a valuable asset in uncertain markets. Businesses should focus on attracting top talent, investing in employee development, and fostering a culture of engagement and collaboration. Empowered and motivated employees are more likely to embrace change, drive innovation, and contribute to the company's success.

Continuous Monitoring and Adaptation: Lastly, in uncertain markets, businesses need to continuously monitor market trends, competitive dynamics, and customer feedback. Regular evaluation and adaptation of strategies are essential to ensure they remain aligned with changing market conditions. Implementing performance metrics and feedback loops can help identify areas that require adjustment and facilitate agile decision-making.

Seizing Opportunities: Identifying Undervalued Assets and Market Trends

Seizing opportunities by identifying undervalued assets and market trends is a key strategy for investors and businesses looking to capitalize on potential growth and maximize their returns. By recognizing assets or trends that are currently undervalued or have the potential for future growth, individuals can make strategic investment decisions or adjust their business strategies to take advantage of these opportunities.

Understanding Undervalued Assets:

Undervalued assets are investments that are priced below their intrinsic value, meaning they have the potential to generate higher returns in the future as their true worth becomes recognized by the market. Here are a few examples of undervalued assets and their potential:

Stocks in Undervalued Companies: Some publicly traded companies may be undervalued due to temporary setbacks, market misperceptions, or simply being overlooked by investors. These companies may have solid fundamentals, strong balance sheets, and promising growth prospects, making their stock an undervalued asset. Investing in such stocks can provide significant gains if the market eventually recognizes their true value.

Real Estate: Undervalued properties can be found in certain markets or due to specific circumstances, such as economic downturns or localized factors. These properties may offer long-term appreciation potential, rental income, or the opportunity for renovation and subsequent value appreciation. Investing in undervalued real estate can be a lucrative strategy if the market conditions improve or if the property's potential is realized.

Commodities: Certain commodities, such as metals (e.g., gold, silver), energy resources (e.g., oil, natural gas), or agricultural products, can experience periods of undervaluation. Supply and demand imbalances, geopolitical factors, or economic cycles can lead to temporary price dislocations. Investors who recognize undervalued commodities and have a long-term outlook can potentially profit when prices eventually rebound.

Cryptocurrencies: The cryptocurrency market is highly volatile, which can result in significant price fluctuations. Some cryptocurrencies, particularly lesser-known ones, may be undervalued compared to their underlying technology, potential use cases, or adoption prospects. Identifying undervalued cryptocurrencies requires careful research and analysis, but successful investments can yield substantial returns if the market recognizes their value over time.

Art and Collectibles: Certain pieces of art, vintage items, or collectibles can be undervalued in the market, especially if they are overlooked or underappreciated at a particular time. As tastes change, new collectors emerge, or the rarity of these items becomes more evident, their value can increase significantly. Investing in undervalued art and collectibles requires expertise and an understanding of market trends, but it can be a rewarding asset class for knowledgeable investors.

Identifying Market Trends:

Market trends refer to the general direction in which a particular market or industry is moving. Recognizing emerging trends early can provide a competitive advantage to investors and businesses. These trends can be influenced by various factors, such as technological advancements, demographic shifts, regulatory changes, or consumer preferences. By identifying and understanding these trends, individuals can position themselves to benefit from the growth potential they offer.

Methods for Identifying Undervalued Assets and Market Trends:

a. **Fundamental Analysis**: This approach involves assessing the intrinsic value of an asset by analyzing its financial statements, industry trends, competitive landscape, and economic conditions. By comparing the asset's intrinsic value to its market price, investors can identify potential undervaluation.

b. **Technical Analysis**: Technical analysis focuses on analyzing price patterns, volume trends, and market indicators to identify potential buy or sell signals. It is commonly used in stock trading and can help investors identify undervalued stocks based on patterns and market behavior.

c. **Market Research**: Conducting market research helps identify emerging trends, consumer preferences, and market gaps. It involves analyzing data, conducting surveys, and studying industry reports to gain insights into potential growth areas.

d. **Networking and Expertise**: Building a network of industry professionals and experts can provide valuable insights and information about undervalued assets and emerging trends. Attending conferences, seminars, and industry events can facilitate networking opportunities and knowledge sharing.

Benefits of Seizing Opportunities:

a. **Potential for High Returns**: Identifying undervalued assets or market trends early can lead to significant returns on investment. By getting in early, individuals can benefit from the growth potential and value appreciation that comes with market recognition.

b. **Competitive Advantage**: Seizing opportunities allows individuals to stay ahead of the competition by capitalizing on emerging trends. This can lead to increased market share, profitability, and business growth.

c. **Diversification:** Recognizing undervalued assets or trends across different industries or sectors enables individuals to diversify their investment portfolios or business offerings. This reduces risk and provides exposure to multiple growth opportunities.

Risks and Challenges:

a. **Uncertainty and Volatility**: The identification of undervalued assets or market trends is not foolproof. There is always a level of uncertainty associated with future outcomes, and market conditions can change rapidly, leading to potential losses.

b. **Information Asymmetry**: It can be challenging to gather accurate and reliable information about undervalued assets or emerging trends. Market inefficiencies or lack of transparency can make it difficult to assess an asset's true value accurately.

c. **Timing**: Seizing opportunities requires effective timing. Getting in too early or too late can impact the potential returns. It is crucial to strike a balance between recognizing the opportunity and executing the investment or business strategy at the right time.

d. **Overvaluation Risk**: Sometimes, assets or trends that appear undervalued may turn out to be overvalued upon closer examination. It is important to conduct thorough research and analysis to avoid investing in assets that are artificially inflated or experiencing a temporary surge in value.

e. **Lack of Liquidity**: Undervalued assets may suffer from a lack of liquidity, meaning there may be limited buyers or sellers in the market. This can make it challenging to exit or realize the investment at the desired price.

f. **Regulatory and Legal Risks**: Investing in undervalued assets or capitalizing on emerging market trends can come with regulatory and legal risks. Changes in regulations, compliance issues, or legal disputes can impact the value and viability of the investment.

g. **Competitive Pressures**: When identifying undervalued assets or market trends, it is essential to consider the competitive landscape. Other investors and businesses may have the same insights, leading to increased competition and potential price escalation.

h. **Misinterpretation of Data**: Interpreting market data, financial statements, or industry trends incorrectly can lead to flawed investment decisions. It is crucial to have a sound understanding of the relevant data and to use appropriate analysis techniques to avoid misjudgment.

Strategies for Seizing Opportunities:

a. **Patience and Long-term Outlook:** Identifying undervalued assets or emerging trends requires patience and a long-term perspective. It may take time for the market to recognize their value, and short-term fluctuations should not deter investors from their original assessment.

b. **Risk Management**: Diversification and risk management strategies should be employed to mitigate potential losses. Spreading investments across different assets or sectors can reduce the impact of individual investment failures.

c. Continuous Learning and Adaptability: Markets and trends are constantly evolving. Staying informed, continuously learning, and adapting to new information and market dynamics are crucial for successfully seizing opportunities.

d. Collaboration and Expertise: Collaborating with experts, industry professionals, or financial advisors can provide valuable insights and expertise in identifying undervalued assets or market trends. Their knowledge and experience can enhance the decision-making process.

e. Thorough Research and Analysis: Conducting comprehensive research and analysis is fundamental to identify undervalued assets or market trends. This includes studying financial data, industry reports, market research, and other relevant information to make informed decisions.

.

Timing the Market: The Art of Identifying Entry and Exit Points

Timing the market refers to the practice of trying to identify the most opportune moments to enter or exit investment positions in order to maximize profits or minimize losses. It is often considered the Holy Grail of investing, as successful market timing can lead to significant financial gains. However, it is important to note that market timing is extremely challenging and can be a risky strategy if not executed properly.

The concept of timing the market is based on the belief that financial markets exhibit certain patterns or trends that can be exploited to generate superior returns. Proponents of market timing argue that by accurately predicting market movements, investors can buy securities at low points and sell them at high points, resulting in higher overall returns compared to a buy-and-hold strategy.

There are two main aspects to timing the market: identifying entry points and exit points.

Identifying Entry Points:
Timing the market to identify entry points involves determining when it is advantageous to buy securities. This can be done using various strategies, including technical analysis, fundamental analysis, and sentiment analysis.

Technical analysis:

Technical analysis is a method used by traders and investors to analyze market data, such as price charts and volume indicators, to identify patterns, trends, and potential entry points for trading or investing in financial markets. The goal of technical analysis is to predict future price movements based on historical price and volume data. While it has its limitations and critics, many traders use technical analysis as a tool to make informed trading decisions.

Here is a comprehensive discussion of technical analysis and how it can be used to time the market and identify entry points:

Price Patterns:
Technical analysts study various price patterns on charts to identify potential entry points. These patterns can be simple, such as support and resistance levels, trendlines, and chart formations like triangles, flags, and head-and-shoulders patterns. By recognizing these patterns, traders can anticipate future price movements and make decisions accordingly. For example, if a stock price has repeatedly bounced off a support level, it may indicate a good entry point to buy.

Trend Analysis:
Trend analysis is a fundamental aspect of technical analysis. Traders identify the direction of the market or a specific stock by analyzing trendlines, moving averages, and trend indicators like the Average Directional Index (ADX). If an asset is in an uptrend, traders may look for buying opportunities on pullbacks or when the price breaks above a resistance level. Conversely, in a downtrend, traders may seek short-selling opportunities or wait for a bounce before going long.

Technical Indicators:
Technical indicators are mathematical calculations derived from price and volume data. They help traders assess market conditions and identify potential entry and exit points. Some commonly used indicators include Moving Averages (MA), Relative Strength Index (RSI), Moving Average Convergence Divergence (MACD), and

Stochastic Oscillator. Traders use these indicators to generate trading signals, such as oversold or overbought conditions, bullish or bearish crossovers, or divergences between price and indicators.

Volume Analysis:
Volume is an essential component of technical analysis. Traders analyze volume data to assess the strength of price movements and confirm the validity of trends. Increasing volume during an uptrend or decreasing volume during a downtrend may indicate the continuation of the trend. Unusual spikes in volume can signal significant market activity, such as the entrance of institutional investors or news events, which could present potential entry points.

Support and Resistance Levels:
Support and resistance levels are price levels where a stock or market has historically had difficulty moving below or above,

respectively. These levels are identified by analyzing historical price data and are often key reference points for traders. When the price approaches a support level, it may present a potential entry point for buying, as there is expected buying pressure. Conversely, when the price approaches a resistance level, it may indicate a potential entry point for short-selling or taking profits.

Fibonacci Retracement:
Fibonacci retracement is a technical analysis tool based on the Fibonacci sequence. Traders use this tool to identify potential support and resistance levels by plotting horizontal lines at specific Fibonacci ratios (38.2%, 50%, and 61.8%) on a price chart. These levels are believed to indicate where the price might reverse or consolidate before continuing in the direction of the trend.

Chart Timeframes:

Traders use various chart timeframes, such as daily, weekly, or intraday charts, to analyze price movements. Longer timeframes provide a broader perspective on the market trend, while shorter timeframes offer more detailed information for short-term trading. Traders may use multiple timeframes to confirm signals and identify entry points with better precision. For example, if a daily chart shows an uptrend, a trader may switch to an hourly chart to find an entry point with favorable risk-reward characteristics

Fundamental analysis:

Fundamental analysis is a method used to evaluate the intrinsic value of an asset, such as stocks, bonds, or commodities, by examining various factors that can influence its price. While timing the market to identify entry points is challenging and often involves a degree of uncertainty, fundamental analysis can provide valuable insights to investors seeking to make informed decisions.

Understanding Fundamental Analysis:

Fundamental analysis involves analyzing qualitative and quantitative factors that affect the value of an asset. It focuses on the underlying factors that drive the market, including the financial health of a company, macroeconomic conditions, industry trends, competitive positioning, management quality, and more.

Key Components of Fundamental Analysis:

a. **Financial Statements**: Analyzing a company's financial statements, including the income statement, balance sheet, and cash flow statement, helps evaluate its profitability, liquidity, debt levels, and overall financial health.

b. **Economic Indicators**: Examining macroeconomic indicators, such as GDP growth, inflation rates, interest rates, and employment data, provides insights into the broader economic environment and its potential impact on an asset's value.

c. **Industry Analysis:** Assessing the dynamics of the industry in which a company operates helps identify growth prospects, competitive forces, regulatory factors, and technological advancements that could affect the asset's performance.

d. **Company Analysis**: Evaluating a company's competitive position, market share, management team, product pipeline, and other relevant factors helps gauge its ability to generate sustainable earnings and future growth.

Identifying Entry Points:
While fundamental analysis helps determine the intrinsic value of an asset, it does not

provide precise timing for entry or exit points. However, it can assist in identifying favorable entry points based on valuation metrics and market conditions. Here are some practical illustrations:

a. **Valuation Metrics**: Fundamental analysis helps compare an asset's current price to its intrinsic value. If the intrinsic value suggests that the asset is undervalued, it may present a favorable entry point. Common valuation metrics include price-to-earnings (P/E) ratio, price-to-sales (P/S) ratio, price-to-book (P/B) ratio, and dividend yield.

b. **Relative Valuation**: Comparing the valuation metrics of an asset to its peers or industry averages provides a relative perspective. If an asset appears undervalued compared to its peers, it may indicate a potential entry point.

c. **Event-Driven Opportunities**: Fundamental analysis can uncover events that may impact an asset's value, such as earnings releases, product launches, regulatory approvals, mergers and acquisitions, or industry-specific developments. Timely analysis of such events can help identify entry points based on the market's reaction to them.

d. **Contrarian Investing**: Fundamental analysis can reveal situations where market sentiment is overly pessimistic or optimistic, creating opportunities for contrarian investors. If the market has unduly discounted a company's value due to temporary factors, it may present an attractive entry point for long-term investors.

Limitations and Considerations: Timing the market based solely on fundamental analysis is challenging due to various factors:

a. **Market Efficiency**: Markets are efficient to some extent, meaning that information is quickly incorporated into asset prices. This makes it difficult to consistently outperform the market solely by timing entry and exit points.

b. **Uncertainty**: Fundamental analysis relies on assumptions and forecasts, which are subject to uncertainty. Unexpected events, shifts in market sentiment, or changes in the competitive landscape can impact the accuracy of fundamental analysis.

c. **Psychological Factors**: Market sentiment and investor psychology can lead to irrational pricing in the short term, deviating from a company's fundamental value. Emotional decision-making can influence market timing strategies.

d. **Complementary Approaches**: Fundamental analysis is often combined with other approaches, such as technical analysis (studying price patterns and trends) or quantitative models, to enhance timing

Sentiment analysis

Sentiment analysis is a powerful tool used in various domains to extract subjective information from textual data and determine the sentiment or emotional tone associated with it. When it comes to timing the market and identifying entry points for investments, sentiment analysis can be a valuable component of the overall analysis.

Market sentiment refers to the overall attitude or sentiment of market participants, such as investors and traders, towards a particular asset, market, or industry. It plays a significant role in influencing market movements, as investors' emotions and perceptions can impact their buying and selling decisions. By analyzing market sentiment, investors aim to gauge the general mood of the market and identify potential opportunities for profitable trades.

Here's a comprehensive discussion on how sentiment analysis can be used in timing the market and identifying entry points, along with practical illustrations:

Data Sources:
Sentiment analysis relies on textual data, so the first step is to gather relevant data sources. These can include financial news articles, social media posts, earnings reports, analyst opinions, and online forums. The broader the range of data sources, the more comprehensive the sentiment analysis can be.

Preprocessing:
The collected textual data needs to be preprocessed before sentiment analysis can be performed. This involves removing

unnecessary punctuation, stop words, and special characters. Additionally, text normalization techniques like stemming and lemmatization can be applied to reduce words to their root form, aiding in analysis.

Sentiment Lexicons:
Sentiment lexicons are dictionaries or databases that contain words and their corresponding sentiment scores. These scores indicate the polarity (positive, negative, or neutral) of each word. Lexicons can be built manually or obtained from existing resources such as the VADER (Valence Aware Dictionary and sEntiment Reasoner) lexicon.

Sentiment Classification:
The next step is to classify the sentiment of each text document. There are various approaches to sentiment classification, including rule-based methods, machine learning techniques (such as Naive Bayes, Support Vector Machines, or Recurrent

Neural Networks), and hybrid models. The chosen approach should be trained on labeled data to learn the relationships between words and sentiment.

Market Sentiment Indicators:
Once sentiment classification is performed on the textual data, market sentiment indicators can be derived. These indicators provide a quantitative measure of sentiment levels in the market. Common indicators include sentiment scores, sentiment ratios, or even sentiment indices calculated based on the aggregated sentiment of multiple sources.

Correlation with Market Data:
To time the market and identify entry points, sentiment indicators need to be correlated with relevant market data. This can include stock prices, trading volumes, or market indices. By examining historical data, investors can identify patterns or

relationships between sentiment and market movements.

Event-Driven Analysis:
Sentiment analysis can also be used for event-driven analysis, where specific events or news items are analyzed to assess their impact on market sentiment and subsequent price movements. For example, a positive sentiment surrounding a company's product launch or a negative sentiment following an earnings disappointment can influence stock prices.

Visualization and Interpretation:
To gain insights from sentiment analysis, data visualization techniques can be employed. This helps investors identify trends, spot turning points, and make informed decisions. Visualization tools like line charts, heatmaps, or sentiment clouds can be used to present sentiment data in an easily understandable manner.

Identifying Exit Points:

Timing the market to identify exit points involves determining when it is advantageous to sell securities and exit positions. The goal is to maximize profits or limit losses before a market downturn occurs.

a) **Profit Targets**: Investors may set specific profit targets based on their investment goals. Once the price of a security reaches the predetermined target, they sell the position to lock in gains.

b) **Stop Loss Orders**: This risk management technique involves setting predetermined price levels at which an investor will automatically sell a security to limit potential losses. Stop loss orders are commonly used to protect against significant downside risk.

c) **Technical Indicators**: Similar to technical analysis for entry points, technical indicators can be used to identify signals for selling. These indicators can include trend lines, moving averages, or oscillators that suggest a potential reversal or a weakening of the market.

While the idea of timing the market may sound appealing, it is important to recognize its limitations and risks:

Difficulty and Inaccuracy: Predicting market movements with precision is extremely challenging, if not impossible. Markets are influenced by a complex interplay of various factors, including economic indicators, geopolitical events, investor sentiment, and unexpected news. Even seasoned professionals often struggle to consistently time the market accurately.

Transaction Costs and Taxes: Frequent buying and selling of securities to time the market can result in higher transaction costs, including brokerage fees and taxes. These costs can eat into potential gains and reduce overall profitability.

Emotional Bias and Overtrading: Market timing requires making decisions based on short-term fluctuations, which can trigger emotional responses such as fear and greed. Emotional biases can lead to impulsive and irrational decision-making, resulting in poor market timing and potentially significant losses.

Missed Opportunities: Attempting to time the market may cause investors to miss out on potential gains during periods of market growth. By staying out of the market or waiting for the "perfect" entry point,

Navigating Global Events: Geopolitics, Economic Crises, and Their Impact on Investments

Navigating global events, such as geopolitics and economic crises, is crucial for investors as these factors can significantly impact investment strategies and outcomes. Geopolitical dynamics and economic crises can create uncertainty, volatility, and various risks that need to be carefully considered and managed. We will explore the relationship between global events, investments, and the strategies investors can employ to navigate these challenges.

Geopolitics and Investments:
Geopolitical events refer to the political and social dynamics between nations that influence the global landscape. Examples include trade wars, international conflicts, regime changes, and geopolitical alliances.

These events can directly impact investments in several ways:

a. **Trade Policies and Tariffs**: Geopolitical tensions often lead to the implementation of trade policies, tariffs, or sanctions, affecting the cost of imports and exports. Companies with global supply chains may face increased expenses or disruptions, impacting profitability and investment returns.

b. **Political Stability**: Geopolitical risks can arise from political instability or social unrest, leading to economic uncertainty. Investors need to assess the political landscape of countries or regions in which they are considering investments to evaluate stability and mitigate associated risks.

c. **Currency Fluctuations**: Geopolitical events can lead to currency volatility as investors react to political developments. Currency fluctuations impact the value of international investments and can affect returns when repatriating profits or dividends.

d. **Regulatory Changes**: Geopolitical events may result in regulatory changes, affecting specific industries or sectors. Investors need to stay informed about such developments to understand the potential impact on their investments and adapt their strategies accordingly.

Economic Crises and Investments:

Economic crises, such as recessions, financial market crashes, or currency devaluations, can have a profound effect on investments. Understanding the implications of these crises is crucial for investors:

a. **Market Volatility**: Economic crises often result in increased market volatility, which can create significant fluctuations in asset prices. Investors should carefully assess their risk tolerance and consider diversification and hedging strategies to manage volatility effectively.

b. **Sector and Industry Performance**: Economic downturns can impact sectors and industries differently. Some sectors, like consumer staples and healthcare, tend to be more resilient during recessions, while others, like discretionary consumer goods, may experience declines. Investors should evaluate the performance and prospects of different sectors to make informed investment decisions.

c. **Interest Rates and Monetary Policy**: Economic crises often prompt central banks to adjust interest rates and implement monetary policies to stimulate the economy. Investors need to monitor these policy changes as they influence the cost of borrowing, inflation rates, and the overall investment environment.

d. **Opportunities in Distressed Assets:**
Economic crises can create opportunities for
investors to acquire distressed assets at
favorable prices. Distressed debt, real estate,
or stocks can offer attractive returns if
purchased wisely. However, careful due
diligence is necessary to assess the
underlying value and potential recovery of
such assets.

**Strategies for Navigating Global
Events:**

a. **Diversification**: Maintaining a
diversified investment portfolio across
different asset classes, sectors, and
geographical regions can help mitigate risks
associated with geopolitical events and
economic crises. Diversification spreads risk
and reduces the impact of negative events
on overall portfolio performance.

b. **Active Monitoring and Research**:
Staying informed about geopolitical

developments, economic indicators, and policy changes is essential. Regular monitoring and thorough research enable investors to make informed decisions and adjust their strategies as needed.

c. **Long-term Perspective**: Global events often trigger short-term market fluctuations. Taking a long-term perspective and focusing on fundamental analysis can help investors navigate through these volatile periods and avoid making impulsive decisions based on short-term market movements.

d. **Hedging Strategies**: Hedging techniques, such as using options or futures contracts, can help mitigate risks associated with currency fluctuations, market downturns, or specific geopolitical events. These strategies can

Balancing Risk and Reward: Setting Realistic Investment Goals and Expectations

Balancing risk and reward is a critical aspect of setting realistic investment goals and expectations. Successful investing requires a careful consideration of the potential risks involved and the expected returns. By understanding the interplay between risk and reward, investors can make informed decisions that align with their financial objectives and risk tolerance. Here, we will discuss comprehensively the key factors to consider when setting realistic investment goals and expectations.

Risk Tolerance: Understanding your risk tolerance is the foundation of setting investment goals. Risk tolerance refers to your willingness and ability to withstand fluctuations in the value of your investments. It is influenced by factors such as your financial situation, investment knowledge, time horizon, and emotional disposition. A conservative investor may prioritize capital preservation and opt for lower-risk investments, while an aggressive investor may be more comfortable with higher-risk investments in pursuit of potentially higher returns.

Time Horizon: The time horizon for your investments plays a significant role in determining your risk tolerance. Investments with longer time horizons generally have a higher capacity to withstand short-term volatility and can benefit from compounding returns. Short-term goals, such as saving for a down payment on a house in a couple of years, may necessitate a more conservative investment approach, whereas long-term goals like retirement planning can accommodate a more growth-oriented strategy.

Asset Allocation: Asset allocation refers to the distribution of your investment portfolio across different asset classes, such as stocks, bonds, real estate, and cash equivalents. Proper asset allocation is crucial for managing risk and optimizing returns. Different asset classes have varying levels of risk and return potential. Diversifying your portfolio can help mitigate risk by spreading it across multiple investments. The allocation should be based on your risk tolerance, investment goals, and market conditions.

Investment Knowledge: Educating yourself about investment fundamentals and strategies is essential to set realistic goals and expectations. Understanding concepts such as risk and return, asset classes, investment vehicles, and market dynamics will enable you to make informed decisions. It is advisable to seek professional advice or consider investment vehicles that align with your expertise and comfort level.

Knowledge empowers investors to assess potential risks accurately and avoid unrealistic expectations.

Historical Performance and Market Conditions: While past performance is not indicative of future results, analyzing historical data can provide insights into how different investments have performed under various market conditions. Consider historical returns, volatility, and correlations among assets. Additionally, stay updated on current market conditions, economic indicators, and geopolitical factors that could influence investment performance. Realistic expectations should be based on a well-informed assessment of the investment landscape.

Regular Monitoring and Adjustments: Setting investment goals and expectations is not a one-time event. It is crucial to regularly monitor your portfolio's performance and make necessary adjustments as circumstances change. Rebalancing your portfolio periodically can help maintain the desired asset allocation and manage risk. Market conditions, personal circumstances, and financial goals may evolve over time, requiring adjustments to your investment strategy to align with your changing needs.

Long-Term Perspective and Patience: Investing is a long-term endeavor, and setting realistic goals requires adopting a patient approach. Markets can be unpredictable in the short term, and investment returns may fluctuate. It is essential to have a long-term perspective and not get swayed by short-term market fluctuations or chase quick gains. Realistic expectations acknowledge that investing involves both ups and downs and focus on achieving sustainable growth over time.

.

The Role of Technology: Harnessing Innovation for Investment Success

The role of technology in harnessing innovation for investment success is crucial in today's rapidly changing and interconnected world. Technology has revolutionized various aspects of the investment landscape, including research, analysis, decision-making, and portfolio management. By leveraging technology and embracing innovation, investors can gain a competitive edge, enhance their investment strategies, and achieve better outcomes. We will explore the key ways in which technology contributes to investment success and how it is reshaping the investment industry.

Access to Information and Data Analysis:

Technology has significantly improved access to vast amounts of information and data. Investors can now tap into real-time financial news, market data, company reports, and other relevant information from various sources worldwide. Advanced data analytics tools and algorithms help investors make sense of this data, identify patterns, and uncover valuable insights. This enables more informed investment decisions and a deeper understanding of market dynamics.

Automated Trading and Algorithmic Investing:

Technology has given rise to automated trading systems and algorithmic investing. These tools use pre-defined rules and algorithms to execute trades swiftly and efficiently, eliminating human biases and emotions. High-frequency trading, for example, relies on complex algorithms to execute trades within microseconds, capitalizing on small price discrepancies. These technologies enable investors to capitalize on market opportunities and optimize their trading strategies.

Robo-Advisors and Digital Investment Platforms:
Robo-advisors and digital investment platforms have democratized investing by making it accessible to a wider audience. These platforms leverage technology to provide automated investment advice and portfolio management services based on investors' goals, risk tolerance, and preferences. They offer cost-effective solutions, diversification options, and personalized investment strategies. Robo-advisors combine technology with human expertise, providing a hybrid approach that caters to a broader range of investors.

Alternative Data and Artificial Intelligence (AI):

The emergence of big data and artificial intelligence has brought about a new era of investment analysis. Investors can now incorporate alternative data sources, such as satellite imagery, social media sentiment, web scraping, and sensor data, to gain unique insights into companies, industries, and market trends. AI-powered algorithms can process and analyze these vast amounts of data at scale, uncovering hidden patterns and relationships that traditional analysis may miss. This enables investors to make more accurate predictions, identify emerging trends, and discover investment opportunities.

Blockchain and Digital Assets:

Blockchain technology, best known for its association with cryptocurrencies like Bitcoin, has the potential to transform the investment landscape. Blockchain offers secure and transparent record-keeping, eliminating the need for intermediaries in transactions. It enables the tokenization of assets, allowing fractional ownership and facilitating the creation of new investment products. Smart contracts, powered by blockchain, can automate and enforce complex financial agreements. These advancements have opened up new avenues for investment, such as digital securities, decentralized finance (DeFi), and non-fungible tokens (NFTs).

Risk Management and Compliance: Technology plays a vital role in risk management and compliance for investors. Advanced risk assessment models, powered by machine learning algorithms, help identify and mitigate potential risks. Compliance monitoring tools ensure adherence to regulatory requirements and detect any suspicious activities. Additionally, technology provides robust cybersecurity measures to protect sensitive investor information and safeguard against cyber threats.

Enhanced Investor Experience:
Technology has improved the overall investor experience by streamlining processes, reducing paperwork, and offering convenient access to investment services. Online trading platforms, mobile apps, and digital wallets enable investors to monitor their portfolios, execute trades, and access investment information on the go. Furthermore, technologies like virtual reality (VR) and augmented reality (AR) are being explored to enhance investor education, training, and engagement.

Conclusion

Mastering investment success amidst uncertainty requires a combination of knowledge, skills, adaptability, and a disciplined approach. The investment landscape is constantly evolving, and uncertainty is an inherent part of the financial markets. However, by following certain principles and strategies, investors can increase their chances of success and achieve their long-term financial goals.

First and foremost, education and continuous learning are crucial for investment success. Understanding financial markets, investment instruments, and economic indicators provides a solid foundation for making informed decisions. Staying updated with the latest news and trends helps investors identify potential risks and opportunities.

Furthermore, diversification is a key strategy for managing uncertainty. Spreading investments across different asset classes, industries, and geographical regions helps mitigate the impact of market volatility. Diversification can help protect against significant losses and enhance long-term returns.

Risk management is another critical aspect of successful investing in uncertain times. Establishing a risk tolerance level and implementing appropriate risk management techniques, such as setting stop-loss orders and regularly reviewing portfolio performance, can help protect against downside risks and preserve capital.

Moreover, maintaining a long-term perspective is essential. Short-term market fluctuations and uncertainties should not derail investors from their long-term investment strategies. Making emotional decisions based on short-term market movements can lead to suboptimal outcomes. Instead, investors should focus on their investment objectives, time horizon, and asset allocation that align with their financial goals.

In uncertain times, being adaptable and flexible is crucial. Market conditions can change rapidly, and investors need to adjust their strategies accordingly. This may involve rebalancing portfolios, taking advantage of emerging opportunities, or reducing exposure to areas of increased risk.

Discipline is the backbone of successful investing amidst uncertainty. Emotion-driven decisions often lead to poor investment choices. Sticking to a well-thought-out investment plan, even during times of market turbulence, helps investors stay focused and avoid impulsive actions that could harm their long-term goals.

Lastly, seeking professional advice can provide valuable insights and guidance. Financial advisors and investment professionals have expertise in navigating uncertainty and can offer personalized strategies based on individual circumstances. Collaborating with a trusted advisor can enhance investment success and provide peace of mind during uncertain times.

www.ingramcontent.com/pod-product-compliance
Lightning Source LLC
Chambersburg PA
CBHW070433220526
45466CB00004B/1663